Ocean Life

Humpback Whale

By Lloyd G. Douglas

Welcome Books™

Children's Press®
A Division of Scholastic Inc.
New York / Toronto / London / Auckland / Sydney
Mexico City / New Delhi / Hong Kong
Danbury, Connecticut

Photo Credits: Cover © James Watt/Animals Animals; p. 5 © Jeff Hunter/Getty Images;
p. 7 © Brandon D. Cole/Corbis; p. 9 © Jeff Vanuga/Corbis; p. 11 © Kike Calvo/V&W/
The Image Works; p. 13 © Johnny Johnson/Animals Animals; p. 15 © Steve Kaufman/Corbis;
pp. 17, 19 © Flip Nicklin/Minden Pictures; p. 21 © Sanford/Agliolo/Corbis

Contributing Editor: Shira Laskin
Book Design: Elana Davidian

Library of Congress Cataloging-in-Publication Data

Douglas, Lloyd G.
    Humpback whale / by Lloyd G. Douglas.
    p. cm. — (Ocean life)
    Includes index.
    ISBN 0-516-25028-0 (lib. bdg.) — ISBN 0-516-23741-1 (pbk.)
    1. Humpback whale—Juvenile literature. I. Title.

QL737.C424D68 2005
599.5'25—dc22

                                                      2004010162

Contents

Humpback whales live in the ocean.

They live all over the world.

Humpback whales are very large animals.

They have **strong** tails.

7

Humpback whales also have **flippers**.

The flippers help them swim.

Humpback whales breathe through **blowholes**.

The blowholes are on top of their heads.

A group of humpback whales is called a **pod**.

A pod of humpback whales works together to get food.

The whales swim in a circle to **trap** fish.

Baby humpback whales are called **calves**.

Mother humpback whales take care of their calves.

Humpback whales call out to each other.

They make noises that sound like songs.

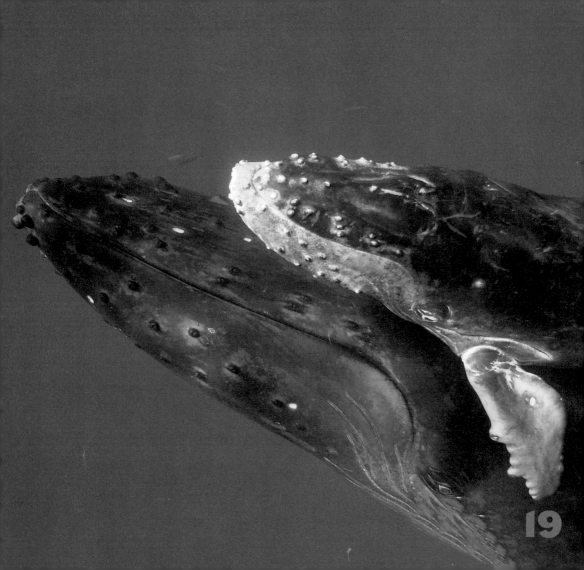
19

Humpback whales jump out of the water.

They are very **powerful** animals.

New Words

blowholes (**bloh**-holz) holes for breathing found on top of the heads of whales

calves (**kalvz**) baby humpback whales

flippers (**flip**-urz) the broad, flat body parts of a sea creature, such as a whale or dolphin, that help it swim

humpback whales (**huhmp**-bak **waylz**) large whales that live in the ocean and breathe through blowholes

pod (**pahd**) a group of humpback whales

powerful (**pou**-ur-fuhl) having a lot of power or strength

strong (**strawng**) having a lot of power

trap (**trap**) to catch someone or something

To Find Out More

Books
Humpback Whales
by Victor Gentle
Gareth Stevens Incorporated

The Journey of a Humpback Whale
by Caryn Jenner
DK Publishing, Incorporated

Web Site
Enchanted Learning: Humpback Whales
http://www.enchantedlearning.com/subjects/whales/species/
   Humpbackwhale.shtml
Read about the humpback whale and play games on this
Web site.

Index

About the Author
Lloyd G. Douglas writes children's books from his home near the Atlantic Ocean.

Content Consultant
Maria Casas, Marine Research Associate, Graduate School of Oceanography, University of Rhode Island

Reading Consultants
Kris Flynn, Coordinator, Small School District Literacy, The San Diego County Office of Education

Shelly Forys, Certified Reading Recovery Specialist, W.J. Zahnow Elementary School, Waterloo, IL

Paulette Mansell, Certified Reading Recovery Specialist, and Early Literacy Consultant, TX